D0722139

THE WORLD OF NASCAR

Building a
Stock Car

By Will DeBoard and Jim Gigliotti

The Child's World®
www.childsworld.com

Published in the United States of America by
The Child's World®
1980 Lookout Drive • Mankato, MN 56003-1705
800-599-READ • www.childsworld.com

ACKNOWLEDGMENTS

The Child's World®:
Mary Berendes, Publishing Director

Produced by Shoreline Publishing Group LLC
President / Editorial Director: James Buckley, Jr.
Designer: Tom Carling, carlingdesign.com
Assistant Editor: Jim Gigliotti

Photo Credits:
Cover: Ken Sklute/Getty Images
Interior: AP/Wide World: 1, 5, 7, 8, 10, 13, 14,
20, 23, 24; Scott Boehm: 16; Joe Robbins: 2, 19,
27, 28.

Copyright © 2009 by The Child's World®
All rights reserved. No part of this book may be
reproduced or utilized in any form or by any means
without written permission from the publisher.

**LIBRARY OF CONGRESS
CATALOGING-IN-PUBLICATION DATA**

DeBoard, Will.
  Building a stock car / by Will DeBoard and Jim
Gigliotti.
    p. cm. — (The world of NASCAR)
  Includes bibliographical references and index.
  ISBN 978-1-60253-073-7 (library bound : alk.
paper)
  1. Stock cars (Automobiles)—Design and
construction—Juvenile literature. I. Gigliotti, Jim.
II. Title. III. Series.

  TL236.28.D425 2008
  629.228—dc22
                                2007049075

Contents

[OPPOSITE]
NASCAR race cars are lined up, ready to hit the road. But how do they get put together before they reach the track? Read on!

Car of Tomorrow

SO WHICH DO YOU THINK CAME FIRST, THE chicken or the egg? Sports fans argue questions like that all the time. For instance: Is Tom Brady a great quarterback because he is part of the New England Patriots' system, or do the Patriots have a great team because Tom Brady is their quarterback? In NASCAR, we could ask: Did Jimmie Johnson win the championship in 2007 because he was the best driver, or was he the top driver because he had the best car?

We can debate those kinds of questions forever. But NASCAR is trying do something about that last one. In 2008, all NASCAR teams began running what is basically the same machine: the "Car of Tomorrow."

The cars still look different on the outside with colorful paint schemes and different logos. Inside, though, they're pretty much the same. The sports term for that is a "level playing field." The winner of a race is the driver who handles his car the best, stays out of trouble, and makes the best strategic decisions. It isn't just the driver who has the best car going into the race.

The Car of Tomorrow—sometimes we'll call it COT for short—sounds like a theme park ride or a video game. For NASCAR, though, the Car of Tomorrow is the car for today. Let's build one—from the ground up!

The Chassis

IF WE WERE BUILDING A HOUSE, WE'D START
with the frame, right? Since we're building a stock car, we'll start in the same place. A car's framework, which is made of steel, is called the **chassis** (CHASS-ee). Think of it as the car's skeleton. Just like you can't see the skeleton of your friend walking around school, you won't see this skeleton after we've finished building the car. Instead, it's under the colorful body. The chassis' main jobs are to keep the car together and the driver safe.

A whole lot of work went into designing the chassis for the Car of Tomorrow. Using computers, designers tried different shapes. They let the computers see how the changes affected the car. The computers were also a great way for the designers to predict how the chassis would perform on the track or in a crash.

Every car has a chassis. But the chassis on a NASCAR car has to be a lot stronger than the chassis on a regular passenger car. At the same time, though, the COT chassis has been specially designed to be flexible in parts, too.

The idea is that those parts will collapse quickly in the event of a high-speed crash on the track. That keeps those parts from injuring the driver.

The part that won't collapse is the **roll cage**. This is the most important part of the chassis. When the driver is racing, he is surrounded by the steel of the roll cage. Ever see a NASCAR crash in which the car spins wildly or rolls over and over—and then the driver gets out, brushes himself off, and walks away? He's safe because of the roll cage. It is made of the strongest steel and is designed to stay in one piece.

On the other hand, the other main parts of the chassis are supposed to collapse in the case of an

Here's the skeleton, or chassis, of a COT being put together. The round bars on the right of the photo form the roll cage for the driver. The square bars on the left will hold the engine in place.

accident. They are the front clip and the rear clip. The front clip supports the front axle and the engine. The rear clip surrounds the **fuel cell**. That's where the gasoline goes, although it's not an ordinary gas tank. It includes protective features that keep the fuel from spilling and causing a fire in case of a crash.

Every piece of the chassis is **welded** to each other piece by hand. Thick steel tubes are carefully arranged to form the shape. The end result looks like that skeleton we talked about. You can see the basic shape, but you can also see right through it.

Next, there are several other pieces to the puzzle. After the chassis has been welded together, several pieces are attached to the car. These parts are made of

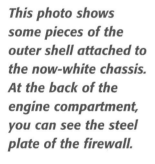

This photo shows some pieces of the outer shell attached to the now-white chassis. At the back of the engine compartment, you can see the steel plate of the firewall.

Not So Stock Anymore

NASCAR stands for the National Association for Stock Car Auto Racing. A "stock car" is one that comes from the stock of a manufacturer. In other words, any person can buy it from the factory (or the dealer's lot). And that's just how NASCAR was when the group was formed to bring some organization to racing in 1948. The cars that its drivers raced were indeed cars straight from the lot. Drivers would work on the cars in their home garages, then drive them to the track on race day, and tape racing numbers on the doors. Then it was pedal to the metal!

Over time, though, NASCAR cars strayed from the "stock" versions of Chevrolet, Ford, and other manufacturers. At first, drivers simply "souped up" their engines, so the cars still looked like stock on the outside. Later, changes began affecting the body of the car, although the manufacturers knew that it was still good advertising to keep them looking similar to their stock vehicles.

With the debut of the Car of Tomorrow, however, NASCAR cars have pretty much completely moved away from "stock"—the COT is different from the factory model inside and out.

thinner sheet metal and include the fender wells, floor pan, and firewall.

The fender wells form the spaces where the tires will be placed. The floor pan covers the underside of the car. The firewall goes between the engine compartment and the driver. The thick firewall plate protects the driver from the searing heat of the engine.

3

Car Bodies

From the adjustable splitter on the front fender to the wing at the back, the COT features many new ways to make cars easier to drive.

JUST LIKE WITH THE CHASSIS, NASCAR OFFICIALS
spent a lot of time designing the body for the Car of Tomorrow. They did their computer work, then made miniature models to test in **wind tunnels**, then made full-sized models for the wind tunnels. After that, of course, cars were tested over and over again on the track. In all, the whole process took more than five years.

Chances are, the finished product doesn't look a whole lot different to you than the NASCAR cars of recent history. Like we said, each team still has its unique color scheme (and car number). And different manufacturers such as Chevrolet, Dodge, Ford, or Toyota still make the front of their cars look a bit like the "regular" cars on the road.

Some of the major changes on the Car of Tomorrow are too small to be noticed at a glance, too. For instance, the COT is four inches wider and two inches

taller than previous cars. The windshield is slightly more upright, too, instead of slanted back as much. And the front bumper is three inches higher and thicker. Those changes might not sound like much. But they make a big difference at the high speeds that NASCAR drivers race. In fact, they help keep speeds from getting out of control—and keep drivers in control of their cars. Even though NASCAR races might be a tad slower in the COT, they figure to be even more exciting, with lots of passing and close finishes!

One change you probably do notice, though, is the new wing on the back of the car. That's another big safety feature. The wing, which can be adjusted up or down as needed, helps direct air down as the car zooms around the track. That's called "downforce" and it helps keep the car securely on the track. There's also an adjustable "splitter" on the front of the COT that also helps control downforce.

The body of a stock car is mainly made up of standard sheet metal. It is handmade by special workers called **body fabricators**. After selecting a flat piece of sheet metal, the fabricator lays a **template** for the COT directly onto it. He then traces around the template's edges with a marker.

The body fabricator uses several types of metal shears, like scissors, to cut the shape from the metal.

All race cars are designed to cut through air resistance smoothly. But their shapes also help "hold" the car down on the track to give the drivers a way to steer safely, even at high speeds.

The piece of metal will then be curved and molded to form the shape of the car. This is one of the most difficult parts of constructing the body. The cut metal is put through two gigantic rollers. As it goes through this machine, the fabricator bends the piece to fit. The piece is then mounted to the car. If it doesn't fit, then the piece might have to be reshaped. Sometimes, the fabricator will have to cut a whole new piece.

When the piece finally does fit, holes will be drilled to insert rivets. These rivets are used to attach the metal

At this point, the outer body, or shell, of the car has been formed from metal, riveted, sanded, and polished smooth.

Other Differences

A lot of things aren't quite as they seem on a NASCAR car. From the outside, the Car of Tomorrow looks like a normal passenger vehicle. But let's open the door or poke our head through a window and see how different it is.

Wait! There are no doors and there are no side windows. The drivers climb in through the window opening. A NASCAR car also has no passenger seat or back seat. These cars aren't built for extra riders. There isn't much comfort for the driver, either, but the custom-built seat helps. A black, nylon netting is placed over the window opening during a race to keep anything from accidentally flying in.

Take a look inside. There is no air conditioning, heater, stereo, cruise control, glove compartment, or horn. Stock cars are built to race, and anything that doesn't help them move faster won't be there.

Walk around the outside. See the lights in front? They aren't really lights. They're stickers that help make the COT look like a regular car.

(The grandstand lights are bright enough that night racing is still possible.) In fact, on most cars, the entire "paint job" is actually a "sticker job." Many of those bright colors on NASCAR cars are stickers, or "skins," that fit like a glove over the body of the car.

That's not the case with Jeff Gordon's famous No. 24 car, though. His sponsor is a paint company!

panels to the chassis. In some cases, there may be as many as a hundred holes in one piece of sheet metal. Stock cars go through intense pounding, so the pieces must be tightly attached.

Once all the rivets are secured, then the body pieces are welded together. The body should be one continuous piece with no visible seams or cracks. The entire body is smooth, too. This is important to help the car cut through the air smoothly and with little resistance. It may take days, even weeks, to get the body as smooth as possible. When the car is traveling at its top speed, even the smallest bump or crack can affect its speed.

Once the body is completely smooth, it is painted with a gray primer to prevent rust. Once the primer is applied, the interior parts will be fitted into the chassis. These parts include the dashboard and the car seat.

Each seat is custom fitted to each driver's body to ensure maximum comfort. There is very little padding such as you would see in a passenger car. As the driver looks around inside the car, he can see the steel tubes of the roll cage. There is nothing else between him and the body of the car.

With the body in good shape, it's time to go under the car. Coming into the garage next are the brakes and the **suspension system**.

Drivers get even more protection from HANS: the Head and Neck Support system. The driver's helmet attaches to a collar over his shoulders, as well as to the seat. This helps keep his head from whipping around dangerously during a crash.

4

Suspension and Setup

IF EVERY DRIVER AND EVERY TEAM IS SUPPOSED
to be using basically the same race car, how does NASCAR make sure they really are? It's through a careful inspection before each race. But like with just about everything else with the Car of Tomorrow, even the inspection procedures are new. In the past, inspections were done with a series of individual templates. Now, though, there's a single grid of templates called "The Claw."

It used to be that teams would spend hundreds of thousands of dollars—maybe even millions of dollars— testing and designing cars to take advantage of the smallest variations allowed in the templates. They would bend the rules as far as they possibly could to take advantage of any gray areas. But with "The Claw," there is no gray area anymore. A car either passes inspection or it doesn't.

What that means is winning and losing a race has even more to do than ever with a car's suspension and **setup**. The suspension is what is underneath the car. It is the system of springs and shock absorbers that affects how the car handles. This system is attached to the wheels and axles. How a driver's crew sets up that system, which is different from track to track, can make the difference in precious seconds.

[OPPOSITE]
Heavy-duty metal springs are placed around the four wheels to help cushion the ride for the driver. Teams can choose different sizes or tightness of springs, depending on the track.

The suspension itself doesn't make a car faster. But it does help the car make it through turns faster. And because every track is unique—for instance, the **banking** on turns varies from track to track—a car needs a different setup for its suspension on every track. In some cases, crews will make hundreds of changes to the setup in the time between races.

The first change to be made in a car's setup is air pressure in the tires. Tires are changed during pit stops in a race. The air pressure can be changed even before the driver makes that stop. The driver is constantly in radio contact with his **crew chief**. He lets his chief know how the car is handling on the track. The chief is the one who then makes the decision regarding air pressure. He directs the crew to prepare the new tires a certain way. Also, because air expands as it gets hotter, tires tend to expand during a race.

Different shock absorbers are also used for each track. Each driver has his own preference when it comes to how a car handles. Shock absorbers have a lot to do with that. For every bump the car drives over, the shock absorber will compress so the driver doesn't feel the bump. At 20 miles per hour (32 kilometers per hour), a bump isn't that bad. But at 175 miles per hour (282 kilometers per hour), a bump could throw a driver against the roof of his car if he isn't wearing a seat belt.

The crew chief is like the head coach of a football team. He is the one who makes strategic decisions during the race. The chief's decisions can be the difference between winning and finishing back in the pack.

Attached to each wheel is a spring. It also keeps the ride smooth. The tightness of the springs greatly affects how the car handles. Tightening or loosening springs is another way teams set up a car.

The last piece of the suspension in the setup is the sway bar. As the car goes into each turn, it wants to roll toward the outside of the track. If you've ever been in a larger car, like a van, you can feel that roll. The sway bar keeps the car from rolling too far to the outside. It can also be adjusted before the race for each driver's needs.

Every NASCAR team is supplied tires from the same tire maker. Taking care of those tires and changing or adjusting them during a race is a big part of the crew's job.

A lot of work goes into setting up a car's suspension. The slightest improvement in a car's handling can mean the difference between winning and losing.

Two other features help the handling of the car: steering and brakes.

The steering wheel is removable to help the driver get into the car more easily. Sometimes you see drivers before a race carrying their steering wheels.

Drivers use the same type of steering wheels at most tracks. Different brakes, however, are used for different tracks. At the longer tracks, brakes are rarely used. At big tracks, the brakes are only used to slow

The cockpit, or driver's area, of the COT isn't that complicated. Drivers keep an eye on a few gauges with a glance. The switches on the left help start the car or control features such as batteries. The red knob on the right is the gear shift.

Tight and Loose

Watch a NASCAR race on television and you're almost sure to hear one of the announcers talk about a car being "loose" in the turns. Or maybe you'll hear a driver tell his crew chief over the radio that his car is too "tight." What do those terms mean?

"Loose" and "tight" help describe how the car is handling. A "loose" car wiggles back and forth as it enters a turn. The back end feels as if it wants to head toward the outside wall instead of properly making it through the turn. A "tight" car isn't turning enough when it goes into a turn. So the front of the car fights making the turn and heads for the wall.

Drivers are very in tune with their cars, and they can **intuitively** feel when a car is too tight or too loose. They'll alert their crew chief, and the team will adjust springs during a pit stop to correct these handling problems.

the car for pit stops, so a lighter system is used. At road courses and shorter tracks, the brakes are vital to success. There, the brakes are used several times during each lap. Considering that the car is moving faster than 100 miles (161 km) per hour through these turns, the brakes need to be heavy-duty.

They also need to be cooled off more often. The friction of braking heats up the brakes so much that you can see them glow red-hot. Some teams will build three extra cooling hoses just for the brakes in these races. These hoses provide liquid for the brakes to cool them.

5

Start Your Engines!

[OPPOSITE]
This big NASCAR V-8 engine looks pretty complicated, right? Well, it is. But NASCAR mechanics know these engines extremely well.

NOW IT'S ALMOST TIME FOR OUR STOCK CAR TO hit the track. First, let's put on four tires. As you might suspect, they aren't just ordinary tires, though. They are special racing tires (see box on page 26). Then, just one more thing: the engine!

One of the engines, anyway. We say one of them because NASCAR teams bring as many as seven engines to each race. With each engine costing about $75,000, that's an expensive pile of metal.

Each engine they bring has its own special job. The qualifying engine is made with lighter parts than a race engine, because a car only takes one or two laps to qualify for the race. Those lighter parts may add one or two **horsepower** to the engine. (Horsepower is a measure of the strength of an engine.) Even though it's lighter, the parts won't break in only a few laps.

A practice engine is usually similar to a race engine. It is used during practice sessions so drivers and crew chiefs can figure out the suspension setup. They don't use their main race engine during practice because they want it to be fresh for the race.

The race engine itself is made with heavy-duty parts because it goes through a lot of stress during a race. After a race, the crew goes over each engine carefully and replaces any part that looks worn. It takes several

Crews use a special crane to lower the engines, which can weigh several hundred pounds, into the engine compartment.

days for a crew to make an engine ready for the next race.

Teams are responsible for their own engines, but they all start with the same basic parts supplied by a carmaker. They put those parts together based on their preferences and driving style, all within the framework of rules established by NASCAR.

Those rules mean that even with different engines, most teams' cars are very close in horsepower: about 750 to 850 horsepower. Compare that to a passenger car engine, which usually generates about 200 horsepower. That's more than enough to power you and your family on the highway. A stock car engine, on the other hand, needs a lot more horsepower.

With all this power, one of the biggest concerns in a long race is keeping the engine cool. The speed in these races can cause the engine to overheat easily. The main cooling system is a combination of oil and water that runs in tubes through the engine. Because of the very high temperatures, only extra-strength hoses are used. Any time a hose fails on the track, it usually means two things. One is that there is suddenly a wet spot on the track that might cause a major wreck. The other is that the engine will usually overheat, ending that driver's race.

Oil also keeps other parts of the car cool. It runs throughout the entire body of the car thanks to a

A piece of paper can end a race! Anything that sticks on the front of the car and keeps air from coming in to cool the engine can lead to disaster. During pit stops, crew members make sure the front of the car is free of litter.

high-pressure pump. Because the oil flows through the entire engine and body, nearly 18 quarts (17 liters) are used. Regular cars use about 5 quarts (4.7 liters).

A small radiator is in place to do nothing but cool the oil. The radiator is mounted in the left front of the car. The air rushing through during the race cools the oil.

Unlike **production cars**, race cars aren't started with a key. Stock cars use a push-button system. Push the

Where the Rubber Meets the Road

The same tire company supplies the racing tires used on all NASCAR cars, but these aren't the same tires that you'll find on your family car. One big difference you can notice right away: There are no grooves on a racing tire. While a passenger car needs the grooves to grab the road, especially in wet or slippery conditions, those grooves would slow down a race car.

A racing tire is also wider than a regular tire. One of the tire maker's best-selling street tires, for instance, is 9 inches (23 cm) wide, compared to 11.5 inches (29 cm) for the racing tire. The racing tire is also about six pounds (2.7 kg) lighter than a 30-pound (13.6 kg) street tire. On the other hand, the street tire has an average life of about 50,000 miles (80,467 km), which means it gets changed every three years or so. A racing tire lasts about 150 miles (241 km)—although NASCAR teams don't even let them go that far. A team will use between 9 and 14 sets of tires in most races.

These tires have put in a good day's work! Look at all the bits of debris and rubber they have picked up from the track.

button, and the car immediately starts up with a mighty roar.

The **drivetrain** includes the car's clutch and transmission. The clutch is a device used to shift gears on the car. Gears help an engine go faster or slower. Most NASCAR drivers don't use their clutch very often. Their clutches are designed so a car can stay in fourth gear—its highest gear—all the way around the track. Only on

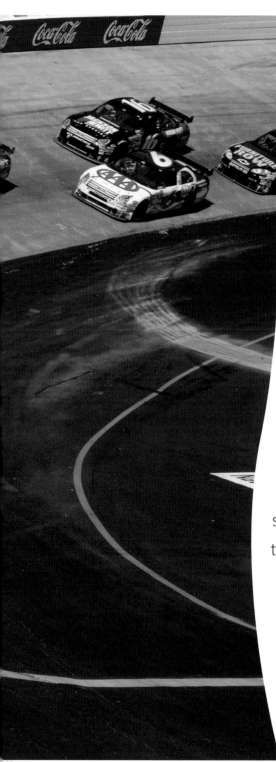

NASCAR's two road courses are clutches used often during a race. On longer oval tracks, the only time gears are shifted by the driver is when he enters and leaves the pit area.

Now the car is ready to race. The chassis has been assembled. The body has been shaped. The suspension has been carefully set up. The engine, brakes, and steering are ready to roll.

Teams go through the same procedure each weekend during the NASCAR season. Sometimes, the body and chassis are in good shape and can go another race, but the suspension and engine will be changed every time.

Then, when the checkered flag waves to signal the end of the race, the team gets ready to do it all over again!

With 43 cars all built the same way, NASCAR races closely match talented drivers in front of thousands of screaming fans.

Glossary

banking   the slope on a racetrack's corners or turns

body fabricators   specialized workers who construct the body of a car by hand

chassis   the steel framework of the car

crew chief   the leader of a race team who supervises team employees and is in charge on race day; the chief is responsible for race-day changes and strategies

drivetrain   the parts of the car—engine, transmission, axles—that link up to turn the wheels

fuel cell   a specialized plastic gas tank for stock cars

horsepower   the unit of measurement by which motors are measured; 1 horsepower is what it takes to lift 550 pounds (249 kilograms) 1 foot (0.3 meters) high in 1 second

intuitively   knowing from a feeling instead of having facts

production cars   cars that are made for public use

roll cage   the frame of steel that protects the driver in accidents

setup   the way something is prepared

suspension system   the system of shock absorbers, springs, and sway bars that affects the handling of the car

template   a shape or pattern used to make the same shape or pattern in another material

welded   connected by using heat to melt two metal parts together

wind tunnels   rooms in which air is pushed over objects at high speeds to see how it moves over those objects

Find Out More

BOOKS

Eyewitness NASCAR
By James Buckley, Jr.
DK Publishing, 2005
This photo-filled book takes you inside the world of NASCAR. See close-up pictures of engines and other gear, meet the heroes of the sport, and see photos of pit-stop and racing action.

NASCAR (Automania!)
By Rachel Eagen
Crabtree Publishing Company, 2006
This book introduces young readers to the world of NASCAR—its cars, history, and drivers.

NASCAR Record & Fact Book
Sporting News Books, 2008
Loaded with facts and figures about current drivers and NASCAR history, this handy reference source also includes details about the Car of Tomorrow.

Pit Pass!
Readers' Digest Children's Books, 2004
Visit pit road, climb behind the wheel of a stock car, check out a team garage, and experience the thrill of race day—it's all in this information-packed book on NASCAR.

WEB SITES

Visit our Web site for lots of links about stock cars:
www.childsworld.com/links

Note to Parents, Teachers, and Librarians: We routinely check our Web links to make sure they're safe, active sites—so encourage your readers to check them out!

Index

aerodynamics, 11, 12, 15

banking, 18
brakes, 20–21

car body, 10–15
car manufacturers, 9, 11, 25
Car of Tomorrow (COT), 4–5, 9, 11–12, 14
chassis, 6–9
clips, front and rear, 8
cockpit, 14, 20
cooling system, 21, 25–26
crashes, 6, 7
crew chief, 18, 21

design by computer, 6, 11
design for safety, 7–8, 9, 12, 14
downforce, 12
driver skills, 5, 21
drivetrain, 27

engine, 9, 22–26
engine compartment, 7, 8

fabricator, body, 12–13
fender, 11, 12
fender well, 9
firewall, 8, 9

floor pan, 9
fuel cell, 8

gasoline and gas tank, 8
gauges and switches, 14, 20
gears and clutch, 27, 29
Gordon, Jeff, 24

handling of the car, 12
Head and Neck Support system (HANS), 15
headlights, artificial, 14
history, 9
"holding" the track, 12
horsepower, 22, 25

ignition, 26–27
inspections and "The Claw", 17
interior. See cockpit

level playing field, 5
"loose" and "tight", 21

models, 11

oil, 25–26

paint job, 14, 15
pit stop, 25

radiator, 26
rivets, 13, 15
roll cage, 7, 15

seat, custom-fitted, 14, 15
shell. See car body
shock absorbers, 18
splitter, 11, 12
spoiler. See wing
springs, 17, 19
starting the car, 26–27
steering wheel, 20
stickers, 14
stock cars, 9
suspension and setup, 16–21
sway bar, 19

template, 12
tires, 18, 19, 26, 27
transmission, 27

welding, 8
window opening, nylon netting, 14
windshield, 12
wind tunnel testing, 11
wing, 11, 12

ABOUT THE AUTHORS

Will DeBoard covered motor sports for the *Modesto Bee* newspaper. He has written articles about NASCAR, lower levels of stock-car racing, Indy cars, and Formula 1.

Jim Gigliotti is a former editor with the National Football League's publishing division. He has written more than twenty books about sports for young readers.

+
629.228 D

DeBoard, Will
Building a stock car
Central Kids CIRC - 4th fl
10/08

DISCARD